THE FACE OF WATER:

NEW AND SELECTED POEMS

ALSO BY SHARA McCALLUM

The Water Between Us
Song of Thieves
This Strange Land

THE FACE OF WATER:

NEW AND SELECTED POEMS

SHARA McCALLUM

PEEPAL TREE

First published in Great Britain in 2011
Peepal Tree Press Ltd
17 King's Avenue
Leeds LS6 1QS
UK

ISBN 13: 9781845231866

Supported by
ARTS COUNCIL
ENGLAND

For Steven
again and always

ACKNOWLEDGEMENTS

"In the Garden of Banana and Coconut Trees", "The Perfect Heart", "The Feast to Celebrate *His Majesty's* Birthday", "jack mandoora mi nuh choose none", "What I'm Telling You", "Sunset on the Wharf", "Jamaica, October 18, 1972", "Persephone Sets the Record Straight", "untitled", "Discubriendo una Fotografia de Mi Madre", "Yuh nuh send. Mi nuh come.", "In My Other Life", "the siren's defense", "I Promise You This", "Calypso", "The Fisherman's Wife", "The tragedy of the mermaid", and "What the Oracle Said" from *The Water Between Us*, by Shara McCallum, © 1999. Reprinted by permission of University of Pittsburgh Press.

"Now the Guitar Begins", "The Story of Tanglehair", "Tanglehair's Mother Speaks", "Tanglehair's Dream", "Big Sister's Lament", "The Story of the Madwoman of the Sea", "An Offering", "The Madwoman Dreams of the Beginning", "The Land of Look Behind", "Autobiography of My Grandmother", "Miss Sally's Wisdom", "Facing It", "Mulatta", "Octoroon Song", "Teresa of Avila (1515-1582)", "Witness", "The Story So Far" and "My Father's Words" from *Song of Thieves*, by Shara McCallum, © 2003. Reprinted by permission of University of Pittsburgh Press.

"Psalm for Kingston", "Dear History ('Believe me when I tell you')", "Miss Sally on Politics", "Election Days, Kingston", "The Waves", "At the Hanover Museum", "Miss Sally on Love", "Dear History ('I could tell when my parents')," "My Mother as Penelope", "Fury", "The Mermaid", "The Shore", "Seagrape", "Penelope", "Gravid Gravitas", "Dear Hours", "A Grammar for War", "From the Book of Mothers", and "History is a Room" from *This Strange Land* © 2010, 2011 by Shara McCallum. Reprinted with the permission of The Permissions Company, Inc. on behalf of Alice James Books, www.alicejamesbooks.org. All rights reserved.

Many thanks to the editors of the following journals, anthologies, and textbooks, in which poems from this collection appeared, often in different versions and/or with different titles: *5AM*, *American Poetry: the Next Generation* (Carnegie Mellon Press, 2000), *American Poetry Now* (University of Pittsburgh Press, 2007), *The Antioch Review, arspoetica (www.logolalia.com/arspoetica)*, *The Beach Book: a Literary Companion* (Sarabande Books, 1999), *Beyond the Frontier: African American Poetry for the 21ˢᵗ Century* (Black Classic Press, 2002), *Bum Rush the Page: a Def Poetry Jam* (Random House, Fall 2001), *Canary River Review*, *Caribbean Erotic: Poetry, Prose, and Essays* (Peepal Tree Press, 2010), *The Caribbean Review of Books, The Caribbean Writer, Chelsea, Columbia, Come Together: Imagine Peace* (Bottom Dog Press, 2008), *Connotation Press: an Online Artifact, The Chattahoochee Review, The Caribbean Writer, Crab Orchard Review, Enskyment, Evensong: Contemporary Poems of Spirituality* (Bottom Dog Press, 2006), *For the Love of Literature* (A.E.L. Publications, Israel, 2011), *Gathering Ground: a Reader Celebrating Cave Canem's First Decade* (University of Michigan, 2006), *Great River Review, Green Mountains Review, Harvard Review, Hubbub, Image, The Iowa Review, Journal of the Motherhood Initiative for Research and Community Development, Luna, Massachusetts Review, New Caribbean Poetry* (Carcanet Press, 2007), *New England Review, Nerve, Obsidian, Ploughshares, Poems of Awakening: an International Anthology of Spiritual Poetry* (Outskirts Press, 2011), *Poetry 30: Thirty-something American Thirty-something Poets* (Mammoth Books, 2005), *Poetry 180: a Turning Back to Poetry* (Random House, 2003), *Poetry Daily, Poui, Prairie Schooner, Review 81: Bob Marley and His Legacy, Role Call: a Generational Anthology of Social and Political Black Literature and Art* (Third World Press, 2002), *Smartish Pace, Step Into a World: a Global Anthology of the New Black Literature* (John Wiley and Sons, 2000), *The Southern Review, Triquarterly, Verse, Virginia Quarterly Review, The World in Literature: 17ᵗʰ Century to the Present: Cultures, Continents, Confluence* (Pearson, Fall 2004), *The Year's Best Fantasy and Horror, Tenth Annual Collection* (St. Martin's Press, 1997), *Zone 3*.

"Susquehanna" was written for the inauguration of Bucknell University's 17ᵗʰ President, John C. Bravman, held on November 14, 2010.

"Dear History" (p. 95) was translated into Spanish by Keith Ellis and published in an anthology of Caribbean poetry in English, *Poetas del Caribe Inglés: Antologia, v. 2* (El perro y la rana, Venezuela, 2009).

"The Land of Look Behind" was translated into Romanian by Mihaela Moscaliuc and published in *Poezia* (Iarna, Romania, 2003).

Thank you to the National Endowment for the Arts for a Poetry Fellowship and to Bucknell University for a leave, both of which enabled the writing of some of these poems.

I am grateful to my husband Steven Shwartzer, my daughters Rachel and Naomi, my other family members, and my friends for their love and support. Special thanks to Terrance Hayes and Mia Leonin, who have been with these poems from the start, to Kwame Dawes, Jeremy Poynting, Hannah Bannister, and everyone at Peepal Tree Press for making this book happen, to Deirdre O'Connor and the staff of the Writing Center at Bucknell University for support and space at a crucial stage with the manuscript, and to Paula Closson Buck, Adrienne McCormick, and Tim Seibles, for their friendship and for weighing-in on some of the selections.

CONTENTS

From *This Strange Land*

New Poems

From *The Water Between Us*

Only the magic and the dream are true. All the rest's a lie.

— Jean Rhys

IN THE GARDEN OF BANANA AND COCONUT TREES

Before the woman's hips
would come to sashay
to other rhythms,
before the man's hands
would grow still, leave
the hollowed-out wood body,
before she would take lovers
over her children,
before his mind would lose
itself to songs
of angels and demons,
before the gospel and herb,

there was my mother,
cooking cornmeal porridge,
plantains, and callaloo for later,
my father's guitar notes,
streaming in from the garden
to hold her singing,
his music, breathing,
lifting leaves
that would collect and stir
at his feet, my mother's
clapping hands, bells jingling
on her ankles.

THE PERFECT HEART

I am alone in the garden, separated
from my class. This is what comes
of trying to make the perfect heart.

Scissors: silvery cold and slipping
through my four-year-old fingers.
I did not know and took the harder route,

tried to carve a mirrored mountain top
from each centre of the page
after page of red construction paper.

Now, I am counting the frangipani
in bloom. Teacher's words still shriller
than the mockingbird's. My cheeks,

wet and hot from more than heat.
If I had been taught, if
once I had been shown the way,

I would have obeyed – not been
a *spoiled, rude, wasteful little girl.*
Folding the paper in two,
I would have cut away the crescent moon.

THE FEAST TO CELEBRATE *HIS MAJESTY'S* BIRTHDAY

When I woke, I could hear them bleating.
All night rain had come down,
grey and steady, over and around our house.
The soil was soft. I could barely hear footsteps
of the men approaching
but knew they had started
by the sound of splintering
wood, the odour of burning grass.

Squinting against the sun, I watched
a caterpillar crawl up the drying banana leaf.
She looked like one I had caught before,
placed in an empty marmalade jar
and fed till she sprouted wings.
Outside, I heard Mummy sweeping,
asking God *how to sing His song*
in this strange land.

When the bleating stopped,
her voice rose above the silence,
ordering me to come help the sistuhs
clean out the goats, saying no picknie
of hers would gwaan like she too good.
Mornings now, I wake in different rooms
to her voice still echoing,
yu hear me? yu hear me gal?

JACK MANDOORA MI NUH CHOOSE NONE

we do not really mean,
we do not really mean,
that what we are going to say is true.
— Ashanti tale

1.

it begins when the mother
            wants rampion   more than her child:
when this weed grows   in the mind   twists itself   into the heart
      causing vanity   to overpower   love

when the father will   consent   to the old woman   to his wife
      not fight to regain   his daughter   himself
            lost   not heard from again

                                    this is where it begins
                                            always
                                    and where it begins
                                            again

when the mother
      would rather have straw
spun into gold   unable
      to turn her face   from the golden light
                        would rather become queen
                        than know the child she will bear

when the father is not present (as before)   obsequious
      to the woman   conceding to her
            by his absence

it is the same story   enchantment
      answers the call of many names:
                        rapunzel   rumpelstiltskin

18

the old granny   locking the child in the tower
            believing
this is the way   you save someone
      climbing up hair   beholding the face
                              of betrayal

the little man whose fingers bleed
      from
      spinning
      gold
                  who returns
                  to the room   thrice
                  offering blood
                  to receive   life

                  other characters not intending harm
                  (the messenger discovering the name
                                    altering destiny
                  denying the little man   the child
                  he would have loved)

fury: stamping yourself into the ground   tearing your body into two parts
            this is the true proof
                  who loves the child   more

19

2.

once upon a time in a land of banana and coconut trees
beautiful princesses married whoever could guess their names
breda anancy was the smartest spider in jamaica: him always fooling
                                        every other creature

mi remember papa
          used to tell plenty stories   about anancy
them always start   with anancy walking down the street
          looking   fi somebody him can fas with

is so anancy stay:
          him always want
                fi push up himself   inna every other person business
                (so we say fas him fas)

                anancy the biggest ginnal mi can think of
                          always tricking people and doing mischief

one time   anancy trick breda gator
          to tek him across the river   and nuh pay him for the trip

another time   anancy trick some creature
          fi give up him magic calabash

                                    much weeping and wailing
                                    and gnashing of teeth did gwaan
                                    after anancy tief way
                                    that magic calabash
                                        lawd it was something fi see
                                    what other thing yu think
                                    could have fill up with nuff food:
                                        bammy and plantain
                                        ackee and saltfish
                                        rice and peas
                                        breadfruit and yam

if yu

did know   the special words

fi call out

calabash   *calabash*   *calabash*

mek it rise up full again

mi grandfather use to tell mi

him nuh know what mek anancy   stay so wutless

that it must be   him just mek that way

whole heap of time   mi would ask mi papa

how anancy   could affect

so many people life

and nuh seem fi care   about him part in it

mi papa say

yu cyan explain   what mek some people

act the way they do

any more than yu can say

what mek things go

the way they go

him say yu must forget

yu musn't want   fi know so much

yu must just accept

things happen that way

jack mandoora mi nuh choose none

3.

in some stories   you have no choice
                                you can't remember
                                            the truth
        it is not possible
                    to go back
                                to uncover
                                            cause
        discover
                    who really
                                is at fault

        so you have to say
                        is anancy do it
            you have to say
                        an evil witch cast a spell
                                forget
                                she was overlooked
                                            not considered
                                            to bless the child
        you have to remember   only
                        the spinning wheel
                        drops of blood
                        light
                        leading the child   from her parents

            then   it is not
                        the mother
                        the father
                                        it is only a story
                        you are trying
                                    to remember
                                            (to forget)

4.

if yu want fi know why
      mongoose nyam up chicken only
     why him so scornful a meat
                   listen carefully:

one time   farmer give anancy and mongoose   them pick of two rope
     fi choose   one of him animal them
              and anancy rope lead him to the fowl

        anancy (being anancy) was vex
           after him mek such a poor choice
              and think up a plan   fi spite mongoose
    (forget se him suppose to be friend to mongoose)

                       tiefing the cow
                   mongoose chose
             anancy cut off the tail
      hide it inna the ground (with one end sticking out)
  and tell mongoose   him cow walk down there
never fi come back
    (same time him offering him chicken to mongoose
          fi mek himself look good)

          now mongoose will only eat fowl meat

no matter   if you was to tell him
                 the truth
take him back   show him   how anancy deceived him
                  it wouldn't matter

     to this day   mongoose   will not hear you
        he will not forgive
           that cow for deserting him

some say
is just a matter of taste
that mongoose grew
unaccustomed   to certain flesh

but i say   is anancy cause it   is anancy mek it   is anancy
who started it

jack mandoora mi nuh choose none

5.

in cinderella
      in snow white
            the mother
                 who lets vanity
                       overpower her

    cannot be   the real mother
                for a real mother   would love her child
                            before herself

    the king   cannot be present
                for a father   (present)
     would protect his daughter

                 (this is how the stories are told
                 this is the way they want you
                 to believe them
                 this is the account offered up
                 as the true tale)

6.

long time ago   when a mother did still love her picknie
            there was a woman name Ma Kayke
                            who had a daughter name Dora

        when the father of the gal gone away   the gal mumma fraid
            fi lef her alone   fraid se some man   would come
                and want fi tief   her precious child away

she lock up the gal inna the house and mek up this song
fi mek her know se is her mumma knock on the door when she come:

                Jack-man Dora, fi mi Dora
                Dora Dora, bring the lock a paley oh!
                Deh Ma Kayke, deh mi here
                Deh Ma Kayke, deh mi here
                Deh Ma Kayke — shwee blam!

            this way   the young gal
        could open up the door   without being fraidy-fraidy

            mi cyan remember all the things that happen
            or how anancy get himself mix up inna this story
    mi only know se   the daughter   and her mumma
                    get separated   by anancy trick

                                long time now
                                mi trying to tell this story
                                to mek some truth
                                whole heap of time
                                mi sit down on mi chair

trying to repeat
                to remember
                        to hear again

to unforget

        to mek   whole

                parts

                      yu understand?

somebody must have cause it   don't it is anancy?

                     him always starting everything

      a beg to ask yu

            if is not anancy   is who?

               jack mandoora mi nuh choose none

7.

granny tells me the story of hansel and gretel:

when they lost their way   in the woods

     trees would not help them
          the moon   only a sliver
               in the night sky
    stars moved
          too quickly   to be guides

               they had to forget
               the breadcrumbs
the mother
       abandoning them
        for her hunger

the father   protesting meekly
       turning back   to his block of wood

   granny says the children   should have loved   the witch

              liquorice
              candy canes
              gingerbread

     were meant for them   all along

   when she asked
      who is nibbling at my house?

they could have answered
      it is us granny: your true children come home

   then   it would have all been different

28

if the children
had remembered
the first journey back:
narrow passage through moonlight
only white pebbles to call

mother   *father*

they would have resisted   wanting jewels
for those who had forsaken them

if the witch had been loved   more
she would never have put hansel
in the cage
having his heart
why would she hunger
for his flesh?

she would never have made gretel
prepare the furnace
gnawing her fingers
like the chicken bone

she would have loved them   (as she had not loved her own child)

saving them
from the axe
chopping steadily
into the silent woods

WHAT I'M TELLING YOU

My father played music. He played a guitar and sang. My father
recorded his songs in the same studio where Bob Marley played
with his band. And if you know who Bob is and are thinking,
"One Love", dreadlocks, ganja, *hey mon,* then you are straying
from the centre of this poem, which is the recording studio where
I slept on the floor while my father sang and strummed his guitar.
And where Bob, who was only a brother in *Twelve Tribes* to me at
four or five, said to the man who called me *whitey gal* that I was
not, that I was a daughter of Israel, that I was Stair's child. That
same Bob who you've seen shaking his natty dreads and jumping
up and down; that same man with the voice of liquid black gold
became a legend in my mind too at four or five as a record
somewhere in a studio in Jamaica started to spin.

SUNSET ON THE WHARF

John crows fill the red sky. Coming in
closer with each swooping pass, they smell

the unsold dead to be discarded. Fishermen,
women with their wares, higglers, pack up

as daylight ends. My father's presence lingers.
With an eight-year-old's eyes, I watch him poised

on one leg, frozen in the midst of motion. Right
leg straight, firmly planted in the soil. Left one

bent at the knee, stranded in mid-air. Walking:
the unfinished step he could not make.

My calling could not retrieve him from that place
he exchanged for me: no *Daddy, Father, Alastair,*

enough to reclaim the eyes averted from my gaze.
What he saw, what he went toward, I was left

behind, pulling at his sleeve as people crowded to see
the spectacle: my father: standing grasshopper,

lotus flower against darkening seas, sand turning black,
grains disintegrating under the dying light of the sun.

JAMAICA, OCTOBER 18, 1972

You tell me about the rickety truck:
your ride in back among goats or cows —
some animal I can't name now —

the water coming down your legs,
my father beside you, strumming
a slow melody of darkened skies

and winter trees he only dreamed
on his guitar. The night was cool.
That detail you rely on each time

the story is told: the one story
your memory serves us better
than my own. I doubt even that night

you considered me, as I lay inside you,
preparing to be born. So many nights
after it would be the same.

You do not remember anything,
you say, so clearly as that trip:
animal smells, guitar straining for sound,

the water between us becoming a river.

PERSEPHONE SETS THE RECORD STRAIGHT

You are all the rage these days,
mother. Everywhere I turn, I hear
Demeter in mourning, Demeter
grieving... poor Demeter.

Always craving the spotlight,
I know this is what you wanted:
your face on the front page
of all the papers; gossip columns

filled with juicy tidbits
on *what life was like before winter,*
old hags in the grocery store, whispering,
how she's let the flowers go,

while young women hover
in their gardens, fearing their hibiscus
will be next on your hit list.
After all these summers,

you still won't come clean.
Passing me iced tea, instead
you ask, *How's the redecorating?*
Are you expanding

to make room for little ones?
Fanning away flies,
you avoid my eyes, saying,
I've so longed to be a grandma,

you know.
For God's sake, mother,
can't you tell me the truth now it's done?
Just once, tell me

how you put me in that field
knowing he'd come,
that you made snow fall
everywhere to cover your tracks,

that the leaves die still
because you can't punish him
for confirming your suspicions:
not wanting you,

he took me instead.
Of course I ate those seeds.
Who wouldn't exchange
one hell for another?

It's always the same. The white house. A little girl who cannot run, cannot scream, can only take apples for kisses, gum for occupying her tongue. It's always the same man, whiteyellowredbrown, his hands larger than her mouth, crackedorsmooth, roughorsoft against her lips. His lap is a hole. If she moves too close, she will sink. She is never alone. Across the room, her sisters sleeporareawake. Down the hall, she can still see them when it grows against her handsfacebetweenherlegs. The mother is never home. Always that same moonorsun staring on. The windows parted. The door ajar. Bathroombedroomkitchen. Always, the same. When she wakes, the moon still in its place. The water on the table.

DISCUBRIENDO UNA FOTOGRAFÍA DE MI MADRE

If I had left Venezuela with you, been on the boat moving
from your world of Papá, Mamá, abuelos, tios, y primos,

I could watch granny cooking en la cocina,
taste frijoles negros y arepas hot on my tongue.

If I had worn your clothes, dressed like this niña bonita
you left behind, I would be able to conjure up the collar

moored to your neck, feel its lace scratching my skin.
If I had the memory you lost to the Atlantic

(the blur of a white house in the background, las caobas
lining the front walk, the music box dancer still spinning

in your hand), if I could do more than imagine you
as this child, I would understand how *tierra*, *pais*,

y casa became untranslatable words. From Spanish
to Patwa, something nameless must have gone wrong.

YU NUH SEND. MI NUH COME.

The first night back and rain falls,
tinging on the aluminium roof.
Trees my tongue had forgotten
return one by one:
      breadfruit, soursop, ackee.

Bougainvillea weigh
with water, fuchsia petals drip
    in disarray.
Love, when you see me next,
    tell me I've changed.

~

If we name in order to know:

    say *apple*
        it will taste red.

    say *bird*
        it will fly
        from your mouth.

    say *home*
        see what stays.

~

In Negril, a bartender asks where I'm from.
    For the hundredth time today I answer:
        Kingston originally.

For the hundredth time I hear:
    Fi true? But yu so light.
        Yu nuh talk Jamaican.

My sister laughs, offering warning:
  Yu better not call her no yankee gal, papa.
   She will get well vex with yu.

Living here again,
  she has the right to say:
   Is fi she country too.

     ~

Long time ago I learned how to mek the ketch arredi grow:
The key is to bruk off a piece from the parent
and plant it inna the ground.

    It will sprout up quick.
    The flower them will come fast
    and grow same way
    as the original tree.

      That's why it call *ketch arredi*.
      That's why it call *never die*.

     ~

From my sister's porch, the airport stretches below me.
Beside it, sea comes in to land,
touching borders of vegetation and sand.

I search for the lizard on the nearby branch,
nearly call Renée to show her it is both there
and not there: so green, you might almost miss it.

All around me, hibiscus and banana trees
fringe the planes taking off. I wonder when they leave,
what assures them they will come down?

IN MY OTHER LIFE,

I was born with a stone in my hand.
My first word was not *mumma*.
I learned from early on that *duppy know who to frighten*
and chose carefully.
I learned to *tell the truth and shame the devil*,
to be seen when not heard,
to spell names of places I would someday know
more than my home:
knife and a fork and a bottle and a cork
that's the way yu spell New York;
chicken in the car and the car cyan go,
that's the way yu spell Chicago.
I took cod liver oil with orange juice each morn.
I ate green mangoes and drank peppermint tea for the bellyache.
I stole otahcite apples from the market.
My hands would not listen and often took licks.
I showed the boys my panty because they said I wouldn't.
I ate stinking toe on a dare.
I knelt down in the dirt and made mud pies.
I climbed tamarind trees, banyan trees, even palms.
I walked barefoot and was not afraid to *ketch cold.*
I tried to catch hummingbirds.
I made bracelets, earrings, and rings from flowers.
I was a queen.
I was a mongoose stealing chicks.
I was a goat on a hillside,
sure of the path.

THE SIRENS' DEFENCE

when we sing
they hear their lives retold
in our song
they see the course
they chose not to chart

it is not our voices
drifting across this ocean
steering them
into these rocks

I PROMISE YOU THIS

Water finds its own level
means your children will know my name.
In the night, when they dream,
fists curled into their face,
the last sound they hear
will be the ocean filling their ears.
Water finds its own level
means you sank low
and quickly into your grave
when you pulled my body ashore,
tore me from my home and left me
calling for air on that scorched beach.
The freak, the half-woman, half-fish
circus attraction, you shrieked.
And not even eternity could stop
the echo of your howling.
Nor can eternity now diminish
my search: your kin, your kin's kin
for every generation to come,
will fear the rush of the tide,
the swell of the wave,
the hint of water
already filling their cribs.

CALYPSO

These days, I don't even bother combing out mi locks.
Is dread I gone dread now.
Mi nuh stay like them other ones, mi love –
with mirror and comb,
sunning themself on every rock,
looking man up and down the North Coast.
Tourist season, them cotch up themself whole time in Negril,
waiting for some fool-fool American,
with belly white like fish,
fi get lickle rum inna him system and jump in.
And, lawd, yu should see the grin.
But man can stupid bad, nuh?
I done learn mi lesson long ago
when I was young and craven.
Keep one Greek boy call Odysseus
inna mi cave. Seven years
him crooning in mi ear and him wife nuh see him face.
The two of we was a sight fi envy. I thought
I was going die in Constant Spring at last,
till the day him come to me –
as all men finally do – saying him tired a play.
Start talking picknie and home and wife
who can cook and clean. *Hmph.*
Well, yu done know how I stay already, mi love.
I did pack up him bag and send him back
to that other woman, same time.
I hear from Mildred down the way
that the gal did tek him back, too;
him tell her is force I did force him fi stay
and she believe the fool. But, lawd,
woman can also blind when she please.
Mi friend, I tell yu,
I is too old for all this bangarang.
I hear over Trini way, young man is beating steel drum,

meking sweet rhyme and calling music by my name.
Well, that the only romance I going give the time of day.
Hmph.

THE FISHERMAN'S WIFE

Each day I will make you
a meal of fish heads soaked
in scallions, scotch bonnets, vinegar,
and wine; cassava pounded flat
beneath my fists, then fried crisp;
roasted plantains; soursop juice
teased with lime. At dusk
before your return, I will
bathe in rosewater, oil my scalp,
polish my skin till it glistens
in the coming moonlight
like mother-of-pearl washed ashore.

In time, you will forget
the painted dusk calling you back;
the surf rupturing herself again and again
for the sand's fleeting touch;
the flamboyant sun rising
from beneath the ocean's shell:
her heat swirling across your face
like Salome's last veil come undone.

THE TRAGEDY OF THE MERMAID

is not that she must leave her home
but that she must cast off her flesh.
To love, she must lose scales as a child
relinquishes dolls to youth;
she must hide the shells
she plants under her tongue,
culling her dreams;
she must stop the tide, rising
in her breath each night;
she must stem the scent of salt
seeping from her skin.
Touching her shrivelled face,
she must not feel an ocean
falling from her eyes.

WHAT THE ORACLE SAID

You will leave your home:
nothing will hold you.
You will wear dresses of gold, skins
of silver, copper, and bronze.
The sky above you will shift in meaning
each time you think you understand.
You will spend a lifetime chipping away layers
of flesh. The shadow of your scales
will always remain. You will be marked
by sulphur and salt.
You will bathe endlessly in clear streams and fail
to rid yourself of that scent.
Your feet will never be your own.
Stone will be your path.
Storms will follow in your wake,
destroying all those who take you in.
You will desert your children
kill your lovers and devour their flesh.
You will love no one
but the wind and ache of your bones.
Neither will love you in return.
With age, your hair will grow matted and dull,
your skin will gape and hang in long folds,
your eyes will cease to shine.
But nothing will be enough.
The sea will never take you back.

from *Song of Thieves*

Won't you help me sing these songs of freedom?
– Bob Marley

Fled is that music.
– John Keats

NOW THE GUITAR BEGINS

1. Last Song

There is a field with no light.
Not the faint shimmer of stars,
not the sliver of a moon.
This night, there is a man
walking guitarless in the grass,
no song in his pocket,
no tune on his tongue. Empty
your voice for him,
it will be no use.
In this field, there is this man
and not even a hint of wind
can stir the tall weeds
through which he moves.
He will lie down, smell
the earth fresh from rain.
He will listen to crickets,
a music he cannot understand.
He will close his eyes.
He will sleep.
He will not get up.

2. A Story

My father thought he was the devil
so he ate an entire chocolate cake —

one my mother had baked —
icing and all, not a crumb left

on the plate. *You must have known*,
he said to my mother. *The voices*

must have instructed you.
A devil's food cake, all for me.

My father thought
he was a god

so he took a broom
to my mother's head

until blood bloomed
on her face, until

her elbow splintered and he saw
what he had done

and it was not good.
Then my father wept.

The voices were a gift.
How could he explain

to one not privileged
to such knowledge?

I walk and freeze mid-step
and must not move at all,

he told my mother,
or the earth will fly apart.

To keep things whole —
don't you see Migdee? —

I must stay still.
Perfectly still.

3. Fate

Nights, my father's voice trawls
the surface of my skin, his rasping
insistent across the gorge of time.

Days, the sound of the sea
is the sound of wind
in the trees, is the sound

of my longing for an end
to this searching
everywhere for his face.

Under the shadow of the banyan,
I see our lives revealed.
Dark and light twinned

within each cell,
I was born with a truth
even he could not bear.

And for that, I have been cast out.
Beloved before any other,
I was once the brightest star

in his heavens.
How does he think —
now exiled — I can live?

4. Electroshock

Imagine it is only light
entering your skin.
Imagine you are submitting
to God's will.

Imagine your body
a fan opening and closing,
fingers like tendrils of seaweed
in an aquamarine dream.

Ask me what it feels like
to break down to your smallest parts,
to feel yourself reduced
to a wind-spray of salt.

Ask me what it means to be
nothing, to be less than even that.
Ask me and I will tell you
because I was there

when the voice filled
the reverberating air,
the moment before it dimmed
and then was gone.

5. *Fugue*

I.

Lemons relinquish their scent
to the breeze.
In the garden, if I could
hold the guitar, its music
thrumming in my hands.
All day the sun
sifts through the trees.

II.

Veins are black birds
clawing beneath skin.
Doctor says to swallow
the pinks, yellows, reds.
But once I heard Jesus
speaking in my voice.

III.

Words are water
slipping through my hands.
Where is Migdalia? So grey,
so blue, her eyes,
like the sky, like the moon
even now
just before dark.

6. *The Call*

At the end of his life, my father stood
at a pay phone in the rain, crying
and calling my mother's name
into the hollow cup of the receiver
mashed close to his mouth,
hair matted, eyes roaming
the distant fields, vacant
without sound. Light
from somewhere beyond the trees
beckoned and he ceased to hear,
only saw a flickering
of birds, angels rustling their wings.

7. Interlude

You are dead
so I wallpaper this room:
white roses for the sound
of your last breath.

I am a flower blooming
out of season: poinsettia in spring,
leaves burning red
long after the last thaw.

In winter, nothing blooms
beneath snow: my breath
on this pane of glass,
white petals of ice.

Death is a chrysanthemum,
the sound of earth covering its face.
You are dead
and I have no breath

enough to call you back:
hyacinth, dahlia, ambrosia,
Alastair, father, son.
The dead have many names

but carry to the grave
the sound of each one.

8. Genesis

In my belly grows a tree.
From that tree, there is light.
In that light, a place
where you are again a son.

Alastair, do branches of this tree
break under the weight
of your shame? Do its leaves
rupture into wounds?

As it was in the beginning
so shall it be in the end,
the body turning back
on itself:

in fear, in love.

9. Music Not Meant for Music's Cage

When I hear you again
fifteen years have passed.
Your throat has long since closed.
I am no longer a bird in your palm.

On this road from Mobay to Negril,
you appear when called: returned
for a moment by the miracle
of recorded song. But after this time

of waiting, I do not recognise your voice,
these words, this song of a thousand birds,
each beating its wings
against the scaffold of my ribs.

10. Coda

So it has come to this:
You have become symbol
of all I cannot name.

Once, I imagined you
a bird, a heron wading through saltwater
marshes, mangroves rooted in sand.

A flush of fish in another dream,
your colours brighter than the possibility
of all reefs.

Or a house on stilts,
out in the shallows of the sea,
whittled by salt, wind, and rain.

The truth I hate to admit
even now is this: I was a child
and you, a man, unreachable

from where I stood
gazing up at your face,
a night with few stars.

I did not know you,
then nor now, anymore
it seems than you knew yourself.

Left with the worst of possible choices —
forgive me —
I made you up.

11. The Flamboyant

The child runs and sand
flaps up in her wake.

He will branch into blossoms
of salt and light.

She does not look back, pressing
her ear to the memory of skin.

His arms grow into the earth,
fingers root in the soil.

Petals rain onto her face.
Sunlight splinters through leaves.

His chest explodes into flowers
of the flame tree, slivers of fire.

THE STORY OF TANGLEHAIR

One day, Tanglehair heard her mother calling and calling. Remembering the pain before, Tanglehair ran far into the woods and found herself in a thicket, caught by her roots. Each strand of hair wrapped fast around the bushes. The more she pulled, the more prickles pierced her scalp. When her mother found her the next dawn, it was too late. All of Tanglehair's twisting and turning left her mother no choice. She cut off Tanglehair's locks to free her.

TANGLEHAIR'S MOTHER SPEAKS

You are the sound of scissors
that will not let me sleep.
You *shrrr* now when you mean
to cry out at night, reminding me
what you have forgotten
as you go about your waking
hours at play.

All day, I watch you grow
away from me: little one,
little once cassava
of mine, you are there still
caught in those woods:
the rabbit, the fawn,
the unborn egg in the nest.
I am the fox, the wolf, the hawk.

TANGLEHAIR'S DREAM

Your voice, like rain
blowing across the fields,
calling me
to come home. I am running
from hands that stalk
my hair. Bushes,
thick; prickles all around
my skin. I am caught
by my roots. Darkness
sinks into me. Inside my flesh
thorns wind themselves
in pathways to my heart.
Mother, I should have heeded
your call. Out here,
wild birds make no sound
like ones I feed from my palm.
Wolves bay in the distance.
The owl cries into the dawn.

BIG SISTER'S LAMENT

I have a little sister, heart
shiny as a brass button.
Smile of a siren,
my shadow self, my
peep-peep cluck-cluck girl.
I take punishments for her.
She laughs when I go
for the bamboo switch,
kisses the salt from my face.
When we play together
she tangles my doll's hair
and I let her, unravel
knots after she's gone.
Now we are grown.
My apple blossom girl,
twilight dancing child,
twirling out of sight.
Heart of alabaster,
heart of close-fisted night.

THE STORY OF THE MADWOMAN BY THE SEA

After walking out of this life, she will paint her toes fire-engine, candy-apple, bright-as-a-kiss-red. She will tie gold-flecked scarves in her hair, each one raining light between her darkening curls. She will wear silver bangles, a dozen pirouetting up and down each arm. Music when she walks. Her former friends will *susu* in corners, whisper of bad genes, madness in the family. Old lovers will creep beneath her window, the room empty but still filled with her body's scent, gardenias blooming beneath snow. They will forget her face, the sound of her voice, remember instead the secret she possessed deep in her wrist, the way she made translucent flesh blush without ever touching skin. One day she will come upon a town and unpack her hair, settle down to watch the coming dusk move across her like the thwarted moon languishing over seashells on the beach. She will plant herself beneath a flame tree, not rise up again. Looking out to sea, she will dream continually of birds, their wings extended over darkening waves and swells. Fuchsia, magenta, chartreuse feathers flash at the edges of sight. Guttural *cawings* issue forth from her beak.

AN OFFERING

I am the woman at the water's edge,
offering you oranges for the peeling,
knife glistening in the sun.
This is the scent and taste
of my skin: citron and sweet.
Touch me and your life will unfold
before you, easily as this skirt
billows then sinks,
lapping against my legs, my toes
filtering through the river's silt.
Following the current out to sea,
I am the kind of woman
who will come back to haunt
your dreams, move through your
humid nights the way honey
swirls through a cup of hot tea.

THE MADWOMAN DREAMS OF THE BEGINNING

From darkness I sprang,
cleaving to the roots of the world,

fashioning myself a dress of weeds,
dried bark from unnamed trees.

In that landscape,
I constituted the fields.

Now when wind rattles
through leaves, you will know me.

A jetty of time,
a flatland of desire,

I rise into mountains, lower
back to meet the sea.

You, who fail to believe,
remember —

before I was,
I was.

THE LAND OF LOOK BEHIND
for D.W.

1. Prologue

In the dark before dawn
cane fields rustle in the wind.

Children sleep, tree frogs
trilling into their dreams.

Across the island, sounds of waiting
echo before the light of morning,

before the cock's crow
opening the sun.

This is an old tale. You say
you have heard it all before.

Then *riddle mi this,*
riddle mi that.

Guess mi this riddle.
Or perhaps not.

2.

Each story dissembles
as landscape.

As they have always done,
women gather at this river,

rinsing laundry, beating sheets
against rocks, wringing them dry

with hands winged and singing,
hands like linen in midday sun,

in afternoon light,
then encroaching dusk.

On the infirmary stoop, eyes clouded
with cataracts, the old man whittled

a piece of wood. How can I say this?
I misunderstood, thought

he was only one more blue-eyed black man
on this island of many — before clarity

emerged, as did the form in his palm,
under the blind weight of memory,

faith:
a shroud I wear.

3.

In my own land,
I have become a tourist,

a visitor *from foreign*. But once,
as a child in my grandmother's garden,

beneath blossoms, I would spin.
The whole world tilted toward me then,

a kaleidoscope of colour and scent.
And I would sing:

Lemon tree very pretty
and the lemon flower so sweet.

But the fruit of the poor lemon
is impossible to eat.

Once many knew the old time songs
of higglers peddling their wares:

She had fill up fi mumma, fill up fi puppa,
Jacob ladder and alligator weed.

Lime leaf, pear leaf, soursop leaf,
sweet broom, cow tongue, granny scratch scratch.

But these tunes have now faded,
taking with them the names of things.

4.

Horse Poison or *Star Flower* —
your other names. *Madame Fate*

when I call,
why do you not answer?

All day I have gone searching
but is only *Love Bush,*

Spirit Weed, and *Shame-o-Lady*
I find. Up and down the hillside

I turn and turn.
But you are nowhere

in sight. Madame Fate,
teach me the lessons of bruised leaves.

Tell me why the heart's scalloped muscle
is enough to stop a lungful of blood.

5.

At dusk, these hills recede into darkness.
First the plum mist of twilight.

Then night settling in, lowering its gauze-
layered skirt on the verandah.

Now is the time of day
when another world wakes

to take this one's place:
crickets loosen their song,

stars chorus in the sky.
Fireflies flicker

to no one in particular.
And only the grass replies.

6.

How long have I loved you
Jamaica of my mind?

Jamaica of the one-one
nutmeg and yam,

the early morning breeze,
the songs caught in leaves:

Pass the dutchie
on the left hand side

and *Hey fatty bum bum,*
you sweet sugar dumpling.

Jamaica of swimming hole waters
so still, so deep, no bottom can yet be found.

How long have I wanted to linger in this place
where seagrapes still litter the shore,

wanted to remain the child
on the strand.

Watch her as she stoops
to lift a husk from the sand.

Turning it over and over in her hand,
she begins the work of assembling –

like a necklace of wounds –
these ruins.

7. *Epilogue*

I had wanted to tell you
a different tale.

I had wanted to be a song,
the dance between

the darkness enveloping us,
the light cobwebbed within.

AUTOBIOGRAPHY OF MY GRANDMOTHER

1. Trinidad

In the dark somewhere
a woman sings, fraying
the edges of my dreams.
Beyond my window,
breadfruit trees
clack their leaves
against the wind.
My mother's face uncoils;
her hands nest in my hair –
all before I discover the sea
between my legs. Then,
we become two,
father is not enough.
Slut. Slut. Slut,
she hisses from her bed
each day I parade
before her gaze.
My white frock never pressed
enough, socks slouching
away from my unscrubbed knees;
my spine curving more each day
despite the doctor's pleas.
Soon, I will be sent to a country
almost at the top of the world.
Early dawn, I walk the path
to Janice's house: Janice
of the mango lips, hips swaying,
mimicking the tide's pull.
Sitting on the verandah,
we hear mockingbirds
begin their calling, women
peddling toward market. She whispers:

don't trust a world covered in ice;
don't trust a world of constant green.

2. Canada

Tonight I leave the window ajar —
snow drifts onto the blanket,
gathering at my feet.
At vespers, nuns' rosaries
are metronomes, suspended
from their waists.
Sister Marguerite leads Hail Marys.
Sister Therése warns:
Keep your skirts down,
your legs shut tight.
All night, the cold enters
my bones. I imagine angels
filling me with their light.

MISS SALLY'S WISDOM

Chiniman say, *Yu put purse on ground,*
yu never have no money.
When yu was not born yet and yu mother
was only a lickle picknie herself,
I did clean people house to mek ends meet.
And when I walk down the street
and some woman standup on her verandah,
chatting whole heap of rubbish,
I just gwaan about mi business same way.
I never so much as miss a step
when I hear her bellow, *Cooyah, but look*
what that woman come to, nuh?

Now to see you like so –
looking like yu lost yu last friend.
Believe me, I understand. I know
what it is to want and not have,
to dream and next thing
yu turn around and, *schwoops*,
yu life done pass already
before yu even think yu start.
So listen good to yu old granny:
Clutch yu purse on yu lap, or tight-tight
up against yu chest. But remember,
wanty wanty no getty getty.

FACING IT

Always the same questions
of blood and bread breaking,
eaten in communion
with what we know — this chair,
the candle flickering.
With what we don't — the dark
outside the window, night
ashen like the voice of my hands.

If I could again be a child
at my mother's side,
I would believe in the stove,
the lit room; in her skirt
swishing against my face
as I crumpled the hem in my fist,
made my hand a flag to wave
my mother's love into my skin.

*I once was lost
but now am found*, she hummed.
And we were, she and I.
And I believed in the night
more fiercely, believed
in my mother, my hand wrapt
in her skirt, moving back and forth
across my face, her face, the face
of God, the face I loved.

MULATTA

First it is like being under water,
floating beneath a stream
of gardenias: the smell
that wants to drown me.

In this shaded light,
in this rippled mirror,
you are one. Touching
the water's cold skin,
you are whole: the voice
of all your longings.

I come apart
like petals falling
from their stem
or being plucked:
one
by one
by one.

In this reflection,
in this place
between shadow and light —
child, say what it is you see.

Then it is like being under water,
only all the time.
That face
that knows my name:
Is it you?
Is it me?

Who plucks these petals
knows your secret.
Whose fingers touch the white underside
of the darkening, flowered skin.

OCTAROON SONG

Blood's the bar I cannot pass
so shield my face from sun,
wear lace and proper trim,
pat my powdered skin
till it glows like mother-of-pearl,
a shade whiter than white.
At night, I dream my hair
curling back, dark
daughters and sons I cannot
risk to bear, swimming
from between my legs.
Ask me my name,
I will say I am damask,
rose-hued and hewn
from divided worlds.
Ask me my name,
I will say I am Eve
and Salome, will say
my face is that place
where continents meet.
Ask me my name
I will answer you
with my father's words,
his language, holy water,
sanctified salvation
blistering my tongue.

TERESA OF AVILA (1515-1582)

When St. Teresa sings
the word blossoms
on her lips, the spine
of the world splinters
into song. When she moves
her hips, she is no saint
but a woman beneath
her cassock, orange as the stain
of the sun. She is not burlap
sacks chafing skin but silken
threads sewn whole.
St. Teresa is the breath
she speaks but
cannot understand:
notes that are sounds,
words divorced
from meaning, only the feeling
of the Latin vowel and consonant
opening and closing
against her throat, a bird fluttering
its wings inside her chest.
St. Teresa is her own redemption,
her body feeding the flock,
her tongue a wafer of its own.
The host, a consecration
of her light, her spirit
and flesh radiating
against the halls of the church,
illuminating its darkest holds.

WITNESS

This is the day you step out
of your car and a child will be
screaming, trying to fit herself
into a narrow matrix
of steel – the space
for shopping cart returns.
Then in the direction
of her gaze – a woman
on the ground, a man above her,
pummelling fists into her face.
Bitch: a mantra loud enough
for you to hear. *Bitch*,
like he knows her,
like she is his. But no,
you understand too late,
a purse torn from her grip – *bitch*,
like give me what I will otherwise take.
You coo to the child, offering
an outstretched hand, and the woman
rises from the pavement, crescent
of blood above her split nose,
in the space between her eyes.
Blood splattered haphazardly
on her face, clothes. Everything
ruined. The man long gone.
The child's hand now shivering
in your own. This day, when you
step out of yourself, out of your own
safe life, into the bright
and natural world.

THE STORY SO FAR

To choose a son for sacrifice
the war continues:

after four thousand years
Isaac and Ishmael still clamouring for God's ear.

In the light of day's end, in a warehouse in Rwanda,
a Hutu foreman hovers over one of his workers,

a pregnant Tutsi woman. This ordinary man
with a wife, children of his own,

will disembowel her. Not a stranger
but this woman he knows. To *learn* —

as later, in his defense, he will confess —
what the inside of a Tutsi woman is like.

On the radio, a young woman recounts her tale
of the Cambodian killing fields:

rice paddies, thatched hut where she plays,
men coming for her father first,

her mother orphaning her so she might survive.
This child eating crickets and coal to stay alive.

Butterflies by the hundreds alight on her face,
cover each inch of skin, their furred wings

opening and closing
against her eyelids, lips, and cheeks.

Told in any language – the parables of suffering,
the fractured syllables of loss,

the space in the back of a throat
still longing to sound the names of God.

MY FATHER'S WORDS

Once I was alone
so my father came to me,
told me the meaning
of flowers that open
by day, close their petals
at night to hide their face
from true light, flowers
that cannot brave
their own darkness.

Once my father was a night
I mistook for salvation,
a voice I mistook for myself.
Once my father
was a bird with wings of longing
and despair, a field of words
blossoming in my ear,
telling me: *my child,*
this is all there is.

from *This Strange Land*

One's homeland is not a geographical convention,
but an insistence of memory and blood.

— Marina Tsvetaeva

PSALM FOR KINGSTON

If I forget thee, O Jerusalem
– Psalm 137

City of Jack Mandora – *mi nuh choose none* – of Anancy
    prevailing over Mongoose, Breda Rat, Puss, and Dog, Anancy
        saved by his wits in the midst of chaos and against all odds,
    of bawdy Big Boy stories told by peacock-strutting boys, *hush-hush*
but loud enough to be heard by anyone passing by the yard.

City of market women at Half-Way-Tree with baskets
    atop their heads or planted in front of their laps, squatting or standing
        with arms akimbo, *susuing* with one another, clucking
    their tongues, calling in voices of pure sugar, *Come dou-dou: see
the pretty bag I have for you,* then kissing their teeth when you saunter off.

City of school children in uniforms playing dandy shandy
    and brown girl in the ring – *tra-la-la-la-la* –
        eating bun and cheese and bulla and mangoes,
    juice sticky and running down their chins, bodies arced
in laughter, mouths agape, heads thrown back.

City of old men with rheumy eyes, crouched in doorways,
    on verandahs, paring knives in hand, carving wood pipes
        or peeling sugar cane, of younger men pushing carts
    of roasted peanuts and oranges, calling out as they walk the streets
and night draws near, of coconut vendors with machetes in hand.

City where power cuts left everyone in sudden dark,
    where the kerosene lamp's blue flame wavered on kitchen walls,
        where empty bellies could not be filled,
    where *no eggs, no milk, no beef today* echoed
in shantytowns, around corners, down alleyways.

City where Marley sang, *Jah would never give the power to a baldhead*
    while the baldheads reigned, where my parents chanted
        down Babylon — *Fire! Burn! Jah! Rastafari! Selassie I!* —
    where they paid weekly dues, saving for our passages back to Africa,
while in their beds my grandparents slept fitfully, dreaming of America.

City that lives under a long-memoried sun,
    where the gunmen of my childhood are today's dons
        ruling neighbourhoods as fiefdoms, where violence
    and beauty still lie down together. City of my birth —
if I forget thee, who will I be, singing the Lord's song in this strange land?

DEAR HISTORY

Believe me when I tell you
I did not know her name

but remember the colour of her dress:
red, like my own school uniform.

I did not know death could come to a girl
walking home, stick in hand,

tracing circles in the dirt,
singing as she went along.

I did not know death
would find someone

for wearing the wrong colour smock
in the wrong part of town.

My parents spoke in hushed tones,
but I heard the story of her body

dragged from street to gully,
left sullied in semen and blood.

I heard the song she sang,
the one I wish I could sing now.

Truth is, I was that girl.
Truth is, I was never there.

MISS SALLY ON POLITICS

He is a one-eye man
in a blind-eye country.

But how him can do better
when no one want to see

what going on. Every time
party man come around

him jumping up and down –
lickle puppy eager fi please.

Him tell mi is not woman
business, this election.

is not fi mi fi understand.
Mi tell yu all the same what I know:

If yu see jack ass,
don't yu must ride it?

ELECTION DAYS, KINGSTON

There are days so long the sun
seems always overhead, a hefted
medallion hanging in the sky.
They sit in the market,
gathering like flies on fruit, linger in dust
kicked up on roads scorched by drought.
They lie on the base of the neck
like beads of sweat stalling on skin.

These are the days in a country's life
when the air is so still
it collects in folds, drapes itself
through the nostrils of young and old;
when the air is weighted with something
approximating hope.

THE WAVES

We walk into rooms that wait for us to enter them.
We walk into waves that threaten to drown us.

But they don't. They fill us instead
with salt, sand, and their own light.

As a child, from a small boat, I watched my father
swim away, ignoring my mother's pleas — her voice

sucked into the wind, my own no match
for the undertow or sharks I feared.

There are moments in a life
when everything comes apart, is ripped so clean

who you are is laid bare. My father returned to us
that day, but he was not the same man

I had seen enter those waves.

AT THE HANOVER MUSEUM
Lucea, Jamaica, 2000

Once many believed in a common dream
of this island, variegated skins of fruit

arrayed at market. *Every mickle mek a muckle.*
But the land keeps opening to loss —

flame tree seeds shaken loose from limbs,
sifted flour that will not rise into bread.

Stalks of cane grow, unaware of their irony,
scattered across this museum's grounds.

Inside, shackles affixed to cement blocks
have rusted to vermillion, almost beautiful.

Here, the sea breaking against cliffs
is a voice I might mistake for the past.

At the entrance to town, the sea wall stands.
Balanced on the edge of water and land,

children play in the surf. Fishermen,
visible in the distance,

will later bring in the day's catch:
snapper on a string, mackerel, even barracuda.

In a place where wind drags through leaves,
where dusk can rip daylight to shreds,

I emerge, remembering
how to eat sugar cane:

spit out the pulp,
before it grows reedy and bitter in your mouth.

MISS SALLY ON LOVE

In my time, I was a girl who like to spree.
The whole world would open fi mi

if I shift mi hips to strain
the fabric of mi skirt, just so.

Still, I did learn mi lesson
where love concern: if snake bite yu,

when yu see even lizard, crawling
with him belly on ground, yu run.

Now the gal come to mi, say she fall in love
with man who have a plan fi change.

But she nuh notice him also carry gun?
And, lawd, how she nuh see

who running the show and who
keeping house same way?

DEAR HISTORY

I could tell when my parents stopped believing.
Marcus, Marley, Manley – their gods

deserted them, leaving little
to wring between their hands.

After a time, revolution's light dims.
Ideals get exchanged for smaller needs,

milk and bread, the crumbs of peace.
In the final days, everyone tried to explain

what had gone wrong: politicians said
tourists would no longer come;

Mummy and Daddy said slavery
was the root; Granny said it was the youth,

killing each other, running wild in the streets.
The night before she and Papa moved to America,

I prayed in the dark of my room
but feared my words

could no longer spiral up to something beyond.
We will come back for you. I promise,

they'd said. When, piece by piece,
my family fled,

we didn't see the bargain
being struck: to live

in a place where memory
becomes a synonym for home.

MY MOTHER AS PENELOPE

Lemon rinds in the dried brook bed,
fireflies failing to light —

all, like me,
suffer the occasional drought.

Outside my window,
no islands of foliage

block my view to the shore.
No river noises trickle in.

Listen, after years of waiting,
I tire of the myth I've become.

If I am not an ocean,
I am nothing.

If I am not a world unto itself,
I need to know it.

THE MERMAID

There is a place where the river meets the sea, where the water turns green and cold and still, a mirror in which you can see into your own eyes but nothing beneath. In Port Antonio, the children walk behind their mother, *peep-peep, cluck-cluck.*

The group descends from the house down the hill, down the winding path scattered with rocks. One of the children recognises the man who sold them bammy and fish last night for dinner and almost turns to wave, but the mother is getting farther ahead.

At the dock, sure footed, she leads the way; the children follow, stepping as if nearing the edge of a cliff. Stopping on the last wooden slat, the mother lifts her dress over her head in one swift motion. At first, the children watch in silence, then begin their protests: *No Mummy. Please don't go.*

Their voices seem to arrive from a great distance. She looks out to the island across the way, decides she will swim to it and come right back.

Through the shade of trees, patches of sunlight turn her naked body into an underwater scene. The children, howling, clench eyes shut; only the trees witness what happens next. Only they see the mother's perfect dive into the waiting depths, the sliver of water opening to take her back.

THE SHORE
for Steve

Then, you turned from me in failing light,
trees startling into sleep,
snow rearranging itself in slender branches.

In the blue air of winter, at dusk,
I stood at the shore in icy reeds,
watching you skate a path across the pond

I was sure would crack when you reached
its centre. The clearing behind the house
opens in memory. Fear

stopped me then as now. Trying
to be brave, to get this right,
I am still the one at the water's edge,

watching the distance between us
grow wider, feeling the thread that binds us
loosen. What happens to love

in such moments? Even now,
as you sit in this morning's light
and I cannot trace the lines of your face,

I struggle to see you clearly:
not the man I love but the man
who is, finally, simply himself.

SEAGRAPE

The first night we travel to his home –
asphalt washed with rain so mist rises,

mingles with streetlamp coronas –
he points out the church he walked to and from

daily for nursery school, the hill
he rode up, delivering newspapers,

sites where I imagine him a boy
I will later love as a man, his past

spilling into our present, winters
that marked him opening again,

a procession of pond hockey games,
drifts of snow I conjure in May air.

When I try to tell him where I'm from,
I begin, *There was a place*

where each sunrise revealed the familiar
outline of the seagrape tree.

When I try to tell him who I am
I start again:

Once upon a time, there was a girl
who reached up through leaves

to pick the seagrape's fruit, and her hair
became entangled in its limbs.

PENELOPE

Long ago I was the vision you needed,
image soldered in the mind's furnace:

girl awaiting your arrival,
watching first light lacerate the sky.

You fancied the sea
a playground for your dreams,

but storms have entered you
like sound enters the skin of a drum,

changing its course.
After years adrift, you return

wanting to know how I exist
apart from you and your myths.

Husband, I learned to bear rupture
by staring down dawn,

to weave as daybreak
split open my rib cage.

Tomorrow when you leave our bed,
the sea's call already filling your ears,

you will find fishermen
hauling in nets, shimmering fistfuls

of fish with bloodied gills. Listen to me:
raise one flopping creature from the rest

to inspect the arc of its dying;
see how struggle inscribes itself on air.

Then say a prayer. Offer a blessing.
Acknowledge your power

to deliver from your palm
whatever life pulses there.

GRAVID GRAVITAS

Then I came to see my body as science fiction,
imagined myself an alien sprouting wings;

craved not pickles but calamari;
devoured tart apples, lemon drops, crystallised ginger;

saw my face, as if for the first time,
reflected back to me in the toilet bowl at 6 a.m.;

suddenly noticed the nasturtium's leaves;
thought I heard grass murmuring beneath my feet;

gazed out windows as my belly rose like baking bread;
swore cinnamon scented the air I walked through;

took myself too seriously, considered myself a delicacy
smoked for days on a spit, succulent and sweet;

bumped into walls and fell down stairs
but landed, cat-like, right-side-up;

invented new words for waiting;
lingered too long on a note;

became the second hand ticking
inside each hour that moved.

DEAR HOURS

1.

We are the body moving toward demise;
we are the soul, remnant of another life.

And always, rain tapping on a zinc roof
is the sound of fingers thrumming flesh.

Always, I return
to the things of this world, tethered.

You, who have come to me
from something, somewhere, I cannot name;

you who have a voice that does not speak
any language I know yet unfurls bright wings,

alighting in each corner of this house;
you who are mine and not mine,

tell me the answers
while there is time.

2.

At Rosh Hashanah, I dip apples in honey,
bargaining for a happy New Year.

I use my teeth to separate bitter from sweet.
I chew on hope, insist its name is faith.

The weight of stones thrown into the river
to cast away sins,

this fruit in my palm whispers *ripening*
in the same breath as *ruin*.

Apple, I say to my daughter, meaning
the thing I wish to be that is not.

Apple, Apple, Apple, my one-year-old parrots,
demanding I place it on her tongue.

3.

Tired, the toddler tiptoes on padded feet.
She pitter-pats on feeted pads.

She whistles and warbles.
She burbles and bobbles.

A slug on its trail of silver,
she slooches down the hall.

A spider dangling from its last thread,
she pauses at the staircase edge.

At eighteen months, what does she know
of danger, the possible fall?

4.

Today your mouth, cheeks, the single curl
escaping your woollen hat

conjure a snapshot of me at your age:
bangled baby, head in a kerchief,

propped on a dark green lawn,
inscrutable gaze taking on the camera.

My snowflake-eating bundle of mischief
and yet-to-be-learned grief,

squealing tangle of two-year-old limbs,
spinning galaxy of self-self-self,

you totter off your sled,
only to resurface a moment later,

as if buoyed by invisible waves.

5.

From the garden, my three-year-old
plucks a zinnia,

almost snapping
the ring of petals off its stem.

At her age, in a different place,
I picked ixoras,

gathering the small blossoms,
one by one, to build a crown of flames.

If I could read my life
backward, or hers forward,

it might begin
the moment the future is written

in a child's need to possess
such a red,

or in her offering
of a flower that will not last

the hour I stand it in a vase,
propping its neck.

A GRAMMAR FOR WAR

After a day when reports of casualties
crackle out of the car radio,

pursuing me as I enter the house at dusk,
eyes wide with seeing,

ears fitted with knowledge
I know neither how to hold nor let drop,

I lay keys on the kitchen table
and scan the air wishing

again I could invent
a lexicon for grief.

If language could recover losses,
words might offer solace

the way a flock of geese follows
a preset trajectory of flight,

the way dawn's arrival restores the ginkgo's
mottled shades of green,

the way the mockingbird sings its song,
conjugating the squandered night.

FROM THE BOOK OF MOTHERS

The smell of your skin fades.
    I forget your heft in my arms,

your hand reaching up to cup my face
    as you nurse, curling into sleep.

Daughter, is it your aging
    or my own I fear most?

~

In fairy tales, the child is trapped
within the refrain: *motherless, motherless.*

In myth, the child is set adrift, left to water's
blind grace, the current's whims.

~

In some part of myself, I remain
    a child behind glass, watching the tall grass

through which my mother drove, the splash of blue
    drawing near. Waiting for the moment

when she decided whose life to save,
    swerving to avoid plunging into the lake.

~

If we are boats, how do we unmoor ourselves, how do we glide?

~

Instructions for a *dai* delivering a girl:

For eighty cents more
      take the newborn child,

hold her by the waist,
      turn her upside down,

give a sharp jerk
      to snap the spinal cord.

Pronounce her
      stillborn.

~

Items for a baby girl:

Tiny bangles for each wrist.
Gold for piercing her ears at birth.

~

Dark Mother, you appear to me
as mad. Mistress of blood, death,

and the death of death,
you surface from the Ganges, pregnant,

stoop to give birth on shore,
then devour your child.

Bearer of destruction, Goddess of Time and Change,
Kali, how can I bring myself to accept your universe?

~

Motherhood: rowing away from the shore.

~

They say:
amniotic fluid is the ocean, blood

pumping to the mother's heart fills the child's ears with first sounds,
the infant knows her mother by smell before sight,

the cord that binds them dies once severed.
They say.

~

Mi navel string bury there.

~

When my sister's first girl came into the world,
she came with the cord wrapped around her neck.

She did not see her mother's face. She did not know
she was loved before she *was*.

~

Mother, I am the dark in your eye.

~

From my grandmother's line
eleven girls have descended, no boys

in three generations.
The women in my family repeat lives:

migrations, madness, exile,
mothers and daughters estranged –

110

connected by a story
that wants to go on without end –

~

Motherhood: the doll whose head refuses to return to its body.

~

I did not hear or could not listen.
      I barely knew you when you called.

Now when it is too late
      I want to tell you I am a mother

and think I understand something
      more of grief's depths. I am a mother

like but also not like you. My friend
      (may I call you this in death?)

my child's throat I
      lean toward to kiss.

~

Motherhood: the promise of feathers against plucking fingers.

~

I will have to admit you – unclaimed woman,
betrayed wife, daughter of the gods, yet exiled.

Prideful one, scorned one, vengeful one –
Medea, your daughters walk the earth, drowning

offspring in bathtubs and lakes,
slashing their children's throats. Medea:

spectre within each of us
who brings forth life.

~

I recite the Hebrew alphabet each time
I must do something my children fear.

Alef Bet Gimel Dalet...

Voice hushed, speech slow,
I repeat these sounds till their breathing stills,

...Lamed Mem Nun...

tears cease, their bodies given over
to a language we do and do not know.

~

Motherhood: the country of want, of want, of want.

~

The old stories had it wrong. Each woman
is within herself mother and daughter, bound

by the same spell. The witch is also she.
So the hag. So too *Old Higue* who leaves her body

nights to visit the child she was in the crib,
suckling the infant's blood to regain her youth,

112

then burning in a brine of flesh
when she tries to return to her skin.

~

If you were a dress, I would wear you, just like my second skin.

~

Force-ripe.
Spoiled fruit.

~

I, Eve, in this boxcar. I, Eve, hearing the wheels
clacking on tracks, the engine's churning. I, Eve,

fitted into the other mothers.
If you see my daughters, tell them –

~

Final note to Demeter:

Bucket, bucket go a well.
Bucket bottom drop out.

~

Demeter's reply:

Bucket, bucket go a well.
Bucket bottom drop out.

~

Pushed from the calabash, stained by its pulp,
we were turned into little girls.

Sent to ease your life, we cooked porridge,
swept the yard, tended goats and fowl.

But the Great Spirit has taken us back,
hearing you curse us: *wutless creatures*.

Returned to oblivion, we have forgotten
the feel of your hands laying us down

by the fire. Where are you, mother,
now the spell is broken?

~

Daughter, I am the dark in your eye.

~

My two-year-old's refrain:

You tell me the answer, Mummy.

~

Dear Mother, Dear M., other, Dear other, my dear other.

~

But here you surface again,
scales glittering in the sun. With a flick of your tail,

I would follow you
to any depths. I would weave a net

114

from my hair, catch fish
for us to feast all day long.

I would stitch your skin with kisses,
reel in the language marooned between us.

But you will never return to me. You,
mermaid in question, of course have gone.

~

What is separation's geography?
The mother's body is the country

of our earliest memory, the soil
from which we are formed.

Our lives are an arc of flight:
away, toward, away.

~

Instructions for lighting candles for Shabbat:

Take the match to each candle's wick. With cupped palms,
pull the light toward you, encircling it with your arms.

Do this three times. Now cover your eyes
to bring the flame inside.

~

Items for mothering:

Thimble, needle, thread.
Three pinches of salt.

~

Make me remember: scallop of flesh, crescent of skin,
　　pulse at the base of her throat.

Help me keep the memory of my girl,
　　stave off her inevitable bloom.

~

Motherhood: the nitty-gritty, the dirty ditty, jingle-jangle, splash, pizzazz.

~

Sing a light song, Mummy.

Twinkle, twinkle –

No the other light song.

This little light of mine –

No. A different light song.

~

Motherhood:

~

If not the tree outside, if not the quiet within,
      if not the coming storm, if not the girl

dressing up in crinoline, the woman
      browning garlic in the pan,

if not this room, this life,
      then where, then when?

HISTORY IS A ROOM

The study of History is the study of Empire.
— Niall Ferguson

I cannot enter.

To enter that room, I would need to be a man who makes
History, not a girl to whom History happened.

Mother to two daughters, I guard their lives with hope, a pinch of
salt I throw over my shoulder.

To enter that room, I would need to wield a gun.

Here, I brandish weapons that serve an art my mother and
grandmother knew: how to make of plantain and eggs a meal.

To enter that room, I would need to live in the past, to under-
stand how power is amassed, eclipsing the sun.

Beneath my children's beds, I scatter grains of rice to keep duppy
at bay.

To enter that room, I would need to live in the present: *This*
election. *This* war.

Beneath my children's pillows, I place worry dolls to ensure their
peaceful sleep.

To enter that room, I would need to bridge the distance between
my door and what lies beyond.

Standing in my foyer at dusk, I ask the sea to fill the crevices of
this house with its breath.

History is recounted by the dead, returned from their graves to walk in shrivelled skins.

In our yard, I watch my daughters run with arms papering the wind.

History is recounted by children in nursery rhymes, beauty masking its own violence.

In my kitchen, I peel an orange, try to forget my thumb must wrest the pulp from its rind.

History is recounted in *The Book of Explanations*: AK-47 begat UZI, which begat M-16... and all the days of their lives were long.

Pausing at the sink, I think of how a pepper might be cut, blade handled so the knife becomes the fruit slit open, its seeds laid bare.

History is recounted in *The Book of Beginnings*: the story of a people born of forgetting.

In our yard, I name the world for my children — *praying mantis, robin's egg, maple leaf* — words for lives they bring me in their palms.

To enter that room, I would need to look into the mirror of language, see in *collateral damage* the faces of the dead.

In our yard, I sow seeds, planting myself in this soil.

To enter that room, I would need to uncover the pattern of a life woven onto some master loom.

Here, I set the table, sweep the floor, make deals with the god of small things.

To enter that room, I would need to be armed with the right question: is History the start of evening or dawn returning the swallow to the sky?

Here, I light candles at nightfall, believe the match waits to be struck.

New Poems

MANCHINEEL

We lived in the house of the slamming doors.
Wind blew into and through each room,

turning our home into a raft, billowing curtains
like sails, setting the four of us adrift.

Our youngest called the place a castle,
she and her sister competing to spy the turret

whenever we rounded the corner,
bringing the roof back into view.

Walking the footpath to the sea,
the children collected rocks, picked weeds

they insisted were flowers, sidestepped the plague
of African snails, entrails splayed and crisping in the sun.

Whole days were spent with each of us lost
inside time's matrices, repeating gestures:

scooping frogs that kept stranding themselves in the pool,
borrowing trinkets from the seabed's floor.

Once wandering the Flower Forest, the children
braceletted their arms and wrists with millipedes.

As if in a dream, my husband and I blindly saw
and smiled. Later when their fingertips flared,

we remembered we'd been given warnings to heed:
avoid the manchineel tree, with its poison apples,

its leaves weeping skin-blistering sap after rain.
Holding their hands, we smoothed ointment

on skin that glowed red for days,
marker of our narrow escape.

WEST COAST

for Dora Sandybird

> *There never was a world for her*
> *Except the one she sang and, singing, made.*
> — Wallace Stevens

1.

Hello darling, she calls,
leaning over a washed-out wooden railing,
standing in lilac dress and grey knitted cap
in full morning light, framed
by a splintering door. Or –
perched on her porch,
gaze absent until someone
enters her view. Then eyes snap back,
an arm extends in greeting.
She descends cement blocks
doubling as stairs with speed
and grace belying her age –
her body becoming
a taut line of longing.

2.

Docked in her yard on emptied oil drums,
a fifteen-foot fishing boat
almost eclipses her face,
her house, the whole of this scene.
Trellising the keel, weeds sprout
lavender flowers, a vine froths white stars,
another – maybe pumpkin –
roots and wraps and climbs, entering
the hull. The wood is rotting,

paint chipping, but a sign stencilled
on one side remains legible:
West Coast,
reminding all who pass this way
exactly where we are.

3.

This time of morning the sun
is a mound of butter, arranged
on a bone china plate.
Beyond her house, the rocky path
opens suddenly unto the sea.
Fuchsia, bougainvillea, desert rose,
and frangipani let go their blooms, petals
browning at the edges.
Her questions chorus:
My father was a fisherman, you know?
You going to the sea?
She is the world, imprisoning
as it consoles: *Alright darling.*
Alright now. You go.

4.

Her mind settles for its own order,
re-sequencing images caught
inside the gears of language, worked-over
by the machinery of illness and age.
Her mind reduces the past
to a smattering of phrases,
looped tape that plays each time we meet:
I had my swim already this morning.
My father was a fisherman.

Mr. Stevens, on some matters we can agree:
there is no world for her
but the one she makes,
compelled by forces
not one of us can fathom.

5.

But about others, I fear now
you were wrong: no one
gets to *sing beyond the genius of the sea*.
Aquamarine dream, original
mystery, the sea closes itself to scrutiny
like pods my daughter collects
on our walks along its shores.
She shakes them and we hear rattling.
But when I split husks
no seeds spill into her cupped hands.
The sea contains its wisdom,
bewitching and bewildering
sailors and fishermen,
their daughters and travellers, alike.

LUCEA, JAMAICA

What I saw there, I could not carry.
She lifted the sheet, revealing the abscess.
I was a young woman then,
travelling toward some notion of home.

Now a sheet had been lifted, an abscess revealed.
I thought I might meet myself,
had travelled home to find
the girl I'd been in braids, lifting a hand to wave.

I thought I might meet her
on this coastal road leaving town.
But another girl, hair in a braid, waved
each day I arrived at the infirmary.

A bend in the road, between tourist towns,
the infirmary was a place you could miss.
Arriving each day, I believed
if I looked long enough I would see

what I'd missed: not the idea but the place itself.
I'd come to a part of my country I hadn't known,
looked long and saw
how liquid pools in opened flesh.

I'd come to a country I'd thought I knew,
a young woman –
liquid, open-fleshed –
and saw what I could not carry.

BIRTH

On the wall, the clock suggests time,
the purview of its ticking

not enough to measure seconds
inside the surgical theatre.

Who in this scene needs saving?
The child? The mother? The doctor

reaches into darkness,
returns with life in her hands,

and the body, broken open, shutters
like the crab burrowing in sand

as the tide recedes, sound
swallowed by the inevitable

silence that follows.

FRACTURE

In the beginning is the girl, body
breaking into promise, each tooth lost
replaced. The girl running ahead, tripping
only when she looks back to see her mother
is following. *Wait*, the mother calls.
Already, it is too late. The future

enters, bones etched with fracture.
I'm almost big as you. See?
Already the narrative is spooling.
Whatever twists of plot may come,
the mother knows her child's story
is one she cannot revise.

HORSE

When the horse came to the window, her master yanked her
back. But in that moment, the child had seen the creature
through nearly opaque glass, their eyes meeting inside the pane's
reflection. Not one adult looked up from her hand of cards or
stopped drinking his gin. They could not anticipate the movement
of the whip, cutting through dense night air, or feel the sting of
the blow that landed on her back. They could not hear cries
carried by the railing wind. When the child was sent to bed,
mother kissed her good night and the darkness of the room
enfolded her. Then, feet tucked beneath sheets, she galloped
across brown fields.

FURY

The madwoman wanders the hall of mirrors. The parrot perched on her shoulder squawks, *Again. Again,* its mantra heeded by no one. The madwoman counts minutes, sees patience as a ticking out of life's losses. In her fingers, she briefly holds each memory before letting her hands fall back at her sides. Now she is no longer a girl running in a garden saturated with lemon trees. She thinks this morning she might be the parrot mimicking language. Or perhaps she has become the single word delivered from its maw.

In the country where she lives, which is no country, the madwoman maps desire's coordinates onto her body. Each hand pressing into her back meets the others that have lingered in that spot; each lover tastes the breath of those gone before, ghosting in her kisses – the madwoman now being all women. The hysteric who cordons off danger so others can believe in safety. The anorectic who starves her flesh so others may eat. The whore whose sex blooms thorns. The mystic whose dust-covered feet discredit her visions. The mother whose placid gaze masks the storm gathering fury into its centre.

AS A YOUNG GIRL THE MADWOMAN CHOOSES EXILE

Walking from the house of my earliest dreams,
I will pass the field where I collected cerasee

mother boiled into tea, will see my birth tree –
its roots and my umbilical cord entwined.

In a new town, I will kneel
at the entrance of the first church I find,

turn my back to parishioners
who mince steps not to sully silks

or tilt their faces toward the sky
to avoid meeting my eyes.

Each day, I will sink my hair into a pail,
taking matted strands to stones laid by men,

scouring the stain of that breath
on the nape of my neck.

SALOME

Back then I was a character in my own life,
daily imagining the possible.

I could be a small pea, clasped
in my fist, or offer my body —

veiled, masking
its multiple skins.

How did I come to stand
in an abrasion of light?

How did I find myself
undressing for others, pivoting ·

to capture any gaze, fasten it
onto my flesh?

Love, if you had seen me when
I was that girl,

would you have recognised me
or turned your face away?

THE MADWOMAN IN MIDDLE AGE

As a girl, I saw the world as mutable –
a beggar could pass for king,

a maiden morph into a fish.
When the caterpillar's husk I clutched

unfolded into wings, I believed
even the dead could return.

I walked across a mountain,
over a sea and an ocean.

For years, I flung salt
over my shoulder to shake

the old people's prediction:
All her life that gal going to suck salt.

I became a woman mistaking
what I'd loved for what I'd lost.

Now, I try not to paint my life
a red that would shame a poppy.

Now, when I watch tea leaves drift
through steaming water,

settling at the cup's bottom,
I tell myself they portend nothing.

THE MADWOMAN AND WATER

Once stepping across algae-covered rocks
I lost my perch and fell, soundless, into the river.

Disoriented, not knowing how to swim,
I did not panic, believing I would stay submerged,

believing the idea only fish could breathe under water
had been a lie, until memory of my short life

on land flooded my lungs. I kicked hard
or was grabbed by hands. Cracking the water's skin,

I came up sputtering. Since then, I have stood
on riverbanks or at the edge of seas, waiting for faith

to return. I have looked into the face of water
to remember how close I came to being birthed

into another world. Silver-skinned,
I would have glittered with such knowledge.

SUSQUEHANNA

I've known rivers ancient as the world and older
than the flow of human blood in human veins.
                                    — Langston Hughes

Landscapes imprint themselves, marking us
with scent — on these banks, pine and humid soil —

with sights we memorise until they become
unremarkable as breathing.

At dawn, mist peels off the water's skin,
then lifts like fine netting, draping

the hills of this valley. Everywhere I look,
the river is present, a scrim for history.

~

Like the migratory shad who begin their trek
each spring when dogwoods bloom, like your origins

in the earth a hundred million years ago or more,
your name is only partly understood:

Hanna, Algonquin for "river" or "stream".
In trying to know you,

I learn of immigrants who entered your story:
Susanna Wright, Joseph Priestley, Aaron Levy, Stephen Smith.

Their lives flare among those of the unrecorded
women and men who landed on your shores.

When they waded through tall grass
and saw asters suspended on ochre stalks,

when they heard a cardinal stutter in the brush,
crows cawing overhead,

did they wonder, as I do now,
Who am I to stand in this place?

~

I stand on the cliff overlooking the confluence
of the river's branches.

I have come to witness its grandeur.
But not much here wants to deliver.

Not the chain-link fence stopping my fall.
Not the butterfly flitting on weeds.

In every direction, hills rim the horizon,
sloping down to muddy water.

Across the surface, a skiff skitters,
spume in its wake.

At this juncture, the current's slight shift
confirms the river's indifference

to our demarcation of North and West,
to bridges connecting island and mainland.

Beauty is part fiction here. I conjure it
by not seeing:

the way as I drive along the river
on Route 15 I blot out

rusting gas pumps,
crumbling farmhouses, and barns;

the way I turn from the wreckage
of human industry to study an oak —

upper limbs steer me toward a sky
so blue it tries belief.

~

In this watershed, time is a pendulum,
swinging backward and forward as the mind directs.

Amish buggies clacking on asphalt collapse
three centuries. Almost.

Steel rails leading from town
signal that other Railroad:

fugitive mother and child racing night,
reversing the river's course

from Columbia into Lewisburg,
where a stable next to the creek and tracks

flickered refuge on their journey north.
Today, a train drags along this site,

trailed by its whistle.
Like that ricocheting sound, memory

wants to invoke the past, asks us to hear
an infant's cries, a mother's hushing reply,

gives body to our wounds,
as if we could commemorate the dead.

~

Here is the river: low from drought, then rising suddenly
when rains swell tributaries and streams.

Here is the river: sluice of acid and rotting herring.
Fisherman casting into a creek so clear

he thinks he can read his fate
in a trout's iridescent skin.

Here is the river, free-flowing and unchecked,
dammed and stilled, interrupted

by islands of cormorants,
egrets, and migratory blue herons,

continuing as it has always done –
carving out rock-faced banks, valleys with loamy fields.

Here is the river: once site of logs
hurtling downstream after winter's floes thawed.

And before: where a Susquehannock woman,
squatting in reeds, stood up,

squinted into the sun to decode the future
assembling on the water.

ABOUT THE AUTHOR

Originally from Kingston, Jamaica, Shara McCallum is the author of three individual collections of poetry, *This Strange Land* (Alice James Books, April 2011), *Song of Thieves* (University of Pittsburgh Press, 2003), and *The Water Between Us* (University of Pittsburgh Press, 1999).

Her poems have appeared in journals in the US, the UK, the Caribbean, Latin America, and Israel, have been reprinted in textbooks and anthologies of American, African American, Caribbean, and World Literatures, and have been translated into Spanish and Romanian. Her personal essays appear in *The Antioch Review, Creative Nonfiction, Witness*, and elsewhere.

She is the recipient of a Fellowship from the National Endowment for the Arts, individual artist grants from the Tennessee Arts Commission and the Barbara Deming Memorial Fund, the Agnes Lynch Starrett Poetry Prize, and an Academy of American Poets Prize, and has been a Cave Canem Fellow and a Walter E. Dakin Fellow at the Sewanee Writers' Conference.

McCallum was on the permanent faculty of the MFA program at the University of Memphis and the Stonecoast Low-Residency MFA program at the University of Southern Maine and has served as visiting faculty for the Catskill Poetry Workshop, the West Virginia Writers Workshop, the Frost Place, and the Chautauqua Writer's Center.

She lives with her family in Pennsylvania, where she teaches and directs the Stadler Center for Poetry at Bucknell University.

NEW POETRY FROM PEEPAL TREE PRESS

Kwame Dawes
Wheels
ISBN: 9781845231422; pp. 205; Pub. October 2011; £9.99

In *Wheels*, Kwame Dawes brings the lyric poem face to face with the external world in the first part of this century – its politics, its natural disasters, its social upheavals and ideological complexity. If these poems are political it is because, for Dawes, politics has become a compelling part of human experience. The poems in *Wheels* do not pretend to have answers, nor are specific political questions seen as especially fascinating. Dawes's core interest remains the power of language to explore and discover patterns of meaning in the world around him. So that whether it is a poem about a near victim of the Lockerbie terrorist attack reflecting on the nature of grace, or a president considering the function of art, an Ethiopian emperor lamenting the death of a trusted servant in the middle of the twentieth century, a Rastafarian in Ethiopia defending his faith at the turn of the twenty-first century, a Haitian reflecting on the loss of everything familiar, these are poems seeking illumination, a way to understand the world.

Dawes frames the sequence around the imagined wheels of the prophet Ezekiel's vision, and then he allows himself the post-modernist liberty of pilfering images from Garcia Marquez's novels, accounts of slave rebellions, passages from the Book of Ezekiel, the current overwhelming bombardment of wall-to-wall news, and the art of modernist painters, to create a striking series of songs that are as much about the quest for love and faith as they are about finding pathways of meaning through the current decade of wars and political and economic uncertainty.

In the end, the poet as prophet knows he is never assured of full illumination or clarity, but the fascinating metaphor of wheels, interlocking and unlocking, provides us with moments of luminosity and sheer beauty.

Loretta Collins Klobah
The Twelve-Foot Neon Woman
ISBN: 9781845231842; pp. 100; pub. October 2011; £8.99

Loretta Collins Klobah gives us a twelve-foot woman with red neon
surging through her veins, who boldly and gracefully takes on the
challenges of urban life. Against a soundtrack of world music, from
salsa to reggae to jazz, and in a vibrant blend of English, Spanish and
patois, she delivers both tender and incendiary hymns of homage to
the Caribbean, America and London.

Scrutinizer, witness, and warner woman, she turns her electric
gaze on the everyday world and its extraordinary people. In poems
that are lyrical, narrative, sensual and often experimental, she
whispers curses against bad-mindedness, sings chants of prophecy,
recites praisesongs to the radiance of rebellion and wails lamenta-
tions for those men, women and children who have been annihilated,
lost or forgotten. There are quiet mediations, too, upon the lives of
girl children, women in precarious situations, older women and
enduring friendships between women.

The world of her poems is urban and aggressively contemporary,
but she sees the enduring presence of splendid, though endangered,
nature and of the spirit-world, which together offer green-hearted
hope for the future and the possibility of cultural metamorphosis.

All Peepal Tree titles are available from the website
www.peepaltreepress.com
with a money back guarantee, secure credit card ordering
and fast delivery throughout the world at cost or less.

Contact us at:
Peepal Tree Press, 17 King's Avenue, Leeds LS6 1QS, UK
Tel: +44 (0) 113 2451703 E-mail: contact@peepaltreepress.com